Hot Metal Tonic

Ron Gavalik

Grit City Publications

Pittsburgh Writer

Published by Grit City Publications
Pittsburgh, PA
Proofreading and Editing: Rebecca Burruss
Cover and Book Design: GCP Contributors

ISBN-13: 978-0692279274 (Grit City Publications)
ISBN-10: 069227927X

Read the Pittsburgh Writer blog
and browse creative services at
PittsburghWriter.net

For the occupiers who refuse to conform,
the tough bitches who don't take shit,
the artists who never sell out,
and the hard-working drunks.
All of you shape the world
more than you know.

Contents

Introduction and Acknowledgements...7

Women and Me..13

Greed and Servitude...33

Political Strife..51

Friends and Enemies..67

Blood is Thicker than Rage...79

Life and Death Everlasting..93

Hot Metal Tonic is the molten form of love and hatred, personal struggle, and whiskey-laced madness. This collection of over 180 poems before you represents a significant contribution to the art form of free verse *MicroPoetry*, a medium born of our social media culture.

The book pays homage to the tens of thousands of steel workers and ancillary tradesmen who once labored in or around the mills that bordered Pittsburgh's three rivers. These blue-collared ancestors of years long past shaped the way I write, the way I pray, and the very way I consider this modern life. The poems here taste of the same gritty soot that once settled in the creviced age lines and moistened lips of the men and women who created the world's metal infrastructure we now take for granted.

Your choice to own and read this collection symbolizes a fearless courage. Delving into avant-garde expression without the safety net of widespread acceptance requires a sense of adventure. You, my friend, are a cut above the average reader, an independent thinker who deserves a congratulatory handshake and a drink.

Writing the entries in this collection took over three years of whiskey-soaked nights as madness crept into my consciousness under the guise of quiet darkness. Amputating one's wretched moments and heartfelt joys from the recesses of the mind, and then converting those memories into verse, is what I'd call a proven form of insanity.

Thankfully, I didn't do it alone.

The people who've agreed to proof, edit, and endorse this collection are formidable literary soldiers. My editor, Rebecca Burruss, is the only person I trust to help shape the direction of my work. Her absolute devotion to the written word is a passion I've not found in any other writer, editor, or publisher.

The opinion-makers and authors who've given their

endorsements of this collection strive to progress their respective crafts to new heights for new generations. I truly respect and adore each of them.

Some have asked, "Why *MicroPoetry*?"

Conformity is a trait that's not usually associated with any aspect of my life. As a child in Mass with my grandfather (pap), I never prayed aloud in unison with the rest of the congregation. Raising a fist of confident protest preceded the correct answer to a teacher's question in school. Working in offices, corporate dress codes often went ignored. As a young father, family members advised the purchase of a stroller and diaper bag. Instead, I carried the boy from place to place and kept his necessities in my writing satchel.

In other words, social acceptance has always been a keen adversary, my arch-nemesis.

Poetry, especially in free verse, is the most expressive and least conformed written art. Combining that kind of individualism with the newer innovation of *MicroPoetry* pushes the literary envelope.

All creativity born of human progress is subject to criticism. The comic strip, jazz music, and silk-screening were all attacked by elitists for not holding to traditionally accepted forms. In historical truth, art is shaped from the grassroots, not from a wealthy master or his overseers.

We are indentured to no one but ourselves.

Poets and experimental writers don't merely punch words onto paper to fulfill a predetermined formula of what mainstream audiences expect. We present new ideas that force new perspectives. We ignite debates among academics. We spark passions in people and launch their imaginations.

In short, we enhance the reader's quality of life.

If only a few people claim to be moved by these passages, I'll have accomplished my goal. All an author can ask for in this world is the occasional fuck, an occasional meal, and the knowledge that his work helps a few working stiffs through their miserable days and nights.

That, my friend, is a sliver of heaven in a world on fire.

Now, kick back, baby.
Open your mind
and allow the hot metal to flow
as soothing tonic.
Prepare yourself
to laugh and think,
cry and rejoice.
Indeed, you will be transformed
into a state of raw emotions.
You and I,
we're about to start a quest,
a journey to memories unseen in years.
Don't worry, it will only hurt so good.
Grasp my calloused hand
and we'll help each other
stumble along this treacherous path
together.

—Ron Gavalik

"some people never go crazy,
what truly horrible lives
they must lead."

-Charles Bukowski

WOMEN AND ME

'I love pie.'
'I love you more than pie.'
'Drop dead.'

Real Woman

You can keep
the hiked-up tits
Give me the woman
who knows how to eat
knows how to love
and has lived through
pain
She's the only one
for me

Molecular Flux

Lovers with soft lips
exit without warning
washed away in summer rain
But their passions
are organic
alive within us
until the final
breath

Seed of Friendship

The doorbell rang
A lonely plate of
steak and potatoes
sat on my porch
wrapped in plastic
Ana stepped inside
her house
She didn't wave

The One Kicked Away

Her humble beauty
and accepting nature
fortified
my embattled heart
I loved her
unconditionally
even when my poor
judgment
lost her
forever

Tortured Desire

Girls in their 20s are sexy
but women over 30
smolder with a
seductive quality
It takes failure
it takes torment
to possess such
allure

For You

I did it all
for you
I walked on water
and on coals
for you
I was your champion
and you left me
for others
many others
I am lost
forgotten

Misconception

'You're leaving?' she said.
'Shut up, cow.'
'Then why did you cum in me?'
He stared at her,
his eyes cold.
'I'm a sinner, baby.
I sinned.'

Nesting

Your need to procreate
does not override
normal human bonding
Take your ticking bio clock
to a dance club men's room
and come home a
mommy

Sperm Shopping

'We need similar goals,'
she said.
'Like what?'
'Marriage. Kids.'
'I just want a girlfriend.'
'What am I?'
I sighed.
'A sperm shopper.'

Control Fail

'I didn't fuck you to get off.'
'I know,' she said.
'I dig you.'
'You wanted to own me,'
she said and formed
an evil grin.
'It didn't work.'

Notice Me

'I have the best tits.'
The world around us faded.
'Wanna see?'
My voice failed.
Her bra dropped.
'You like them?'
Attention before love.

Friday Love

'Romance me,' she said.
'Yeah, ok.'
'Love me, intensely.'
'Sure,' I said, 'for 36 hours.'
'Huh? Why?'
'I need Sunday, baby,
for myself.'

Soggy

'Why are you fat?'
Good men ignore drunken women.
I'm not good men.
'I eat meat, dumb bitch.'
A martini on my head
wasn't a great
accessory.

Misogynist?

'Your mom's crazy, but...'
she bit her lip,
'You hate women.'
I didn't speak.
'Your poems are like rape.'
A man is damned by
interpretation.

The Right Type

'Women are nuts,'
my brother said.
'Date younger.'
'Why?'
'They're not broken,' I said.
'What do they want?'
'Family.'
Now he's happy.

Depravity

Cowards on social media
ask girls for head
or threesomes
It's disappointing
but even worse
when young sluts
thrive on such
sad attention

Resist and Reward

Champions ignore
temptations
of unpredictable sluts
Warriors push past
crooks with legs
and stay on the path
to win the love
of a good
woman

Promiscuity

I've discovered
women who
claim innocence
are lying tramps
attention whores
But honest sluts
are the best lovers
and most incredible
friends

When Words Fail

'I love you,' she said.
'Show me, baby.'
Her tongue stroked a portrait
of raw emotion
onto my flesh.
'I love you, too,' I said,
'forever.'

Necessity

'I need you,' she said
in whiskey-laced breath.
'Me too, baby.'
'I think that's how we know
its love.'
'Yes,' she said,
'the only love.'

Manipulation

'It will hurt so good, baby.'
'Empty promises,' she said.
His face went red and
he drove in hard
to her delight.
Men are simple
creatures.

Toxicity

I never said
it wouldn't hurt
to love a man who hits
The shiners and cuts
will heal
but your broken heart
will always be
imprisoned
with him

Plagued

Through a haze of
tar and nicotine
her lonely hips
swayed next to the bar
The cheap skirt was a
fast score
but her memory
forever
haunts me

Narcissism

The polluted smog of lies
cast upon each other
as we quest for
self-gratification
grows more potent
more poisonous
with each
passing
moment

Salesmanship

Getting a guy hard
is not about fashion
makeup
or a skill
It's biology
Talent is convincing him
to give up freedom
for family life
with you

Romantic Superhighway

Online dating sites
are vain portals
for lonely
wretched souls
We seek validation
that our imperfect
minds and bodies
are worthy
of love

False Esteem

I'm tired of reading
on social media
how women claim
independence
Shut up
You got a job
It's called adulthood
Congratulations
You're boring

Coffee Date

'I love to travel.
Do you love beaches?
I hate Atlantic City.
Do you love Twilight
movies, too?'
At this point,
I prayed for death
or a gun.

20-Minute Hell

'What do you do for a living?' she said.
'I breathe, drink, and eat.'
'I don't get it.'
'Neither do I.'
That was my cue
to split.

Broken Love

Tina smirked behind her ice cream.
'You don't love Gia?'
'Sure I do.'
'She's broken.'
'True.'
'You just love the challenge.'
She was right.

Destitution

'You don't love me.'
'I do so.'
'You just love my ass.'
'Actually, I love your purse.'
'Get out!'
Hardship
is when a man
counts each meal.

Loneliness

There's no hope in a glass
but no one drinks for
empty promises
Whiskey covers loneliness
the hard truth
She will never return
to me

Aggression

If a woman says no
be respectful
But if she hesitates
become an
aggressive champion
Be the man
she respects
she desires
Be the man
she needs

Plunder

I didn't seek consent.
Her false resistance and
deep moans
signified passion.
Afterwards she said,
'You never asked.'
'I never do.'
'Good.'

Ravishment

Calloused fingers spread
her thighs
I slide in
Each angry thrust
is pure hatred
I drive deep
until she is mine
tied to my
evil intentions

Dark Lust

Screwing you
evacuated my soul
as the succubus
drains his victim of life
Your empty hatred
has infected me
until death
do I part

Teenage Standard

'Sex?'
'No.'
'Please?'
'No.'
'Please?'
'No.'
'Please?'
'Ugh.'
'Please?'
'No.'
'C'mon!'
'No.'
'Really?'
'No.'
'Please?'
'No.'
'Now?'
'Ok.'

Paradox

'I wonder how my future ex-wife will hurt me.'
'Screw my past ex-husband.'
'Let's get married.'
'Why?'
'So you two can get back together.'

Midsummer Night

Thunder shook my windows.
Kim pushed against me
in bed.
'I hate storms,' she said.
I held her close.
This time,
with this woman,
I meant it.

Real Devotion

'I'm poison, Ana.'
'If we can't date, what are we?'
'Hetero-asexual-life-partners.'
'What?'
'Loyalty without prison.'
'Oh...I like that.'

GREED

AND

SERVITUDE

Coffee is yummy
Liquid heaven in my mug
The work day begins

Will Work for Food

Working a job
is to perform hateful tasks
that earn the boss
more money
than he'll ever pay
Our choices are simple
conform
starve or
rebel

Welcome to Adult Work

After a week
on the drywall job
I wasn't paid
The boss made excuses
for weeks
Finally
I robbed his truck
and sold his tools
at a swap meet

Retail Revenge

At K-Mart
clerks printed the store name
on fishing licenses
I signed my own name
Fishermen wore my *brand*
pinned to their caps
all summer

Car Wash

I needed cash for diapers.
The boss smelled
my desperation.
'Muck out the floor drains.'
They stunk of vomit.
No one else did it,
only me.

The Wrong Choice

Drafting school
was pure math.
'When do we draw blue prints?'
The teacher sighed.
'This is drawing.'
Truck driving
always looked
like fun.

Telemarketing

You gotta find an angle.
'Renew your magazine?'
'No.'
'You get free hooch!'
Commissions flowed
for a week.
Want ads always
looked the same.

Glamour

Bartending loses charm
when you mop puke
and haul garbage
down a fire
escape
A man has time to think
as he brushes
roaches
from his pants

Comply

Pull on those khakis
You'll blend in
with the herd
They're quite comfortable
once you stop
the futile resistance
and swear
your allegiance

Drafting Career

Overseers watched
as we sweat-shopped
around a long table
If a drawing went over
the time allotted
you were scorned
It took a year
to escape

Forking the Activator

Jeff always wore
the same red tie.
'I hate ties,' he'd say.
Engineers are quirky.
In rebellion,
he named his
new designs after
porn films.

Beacon of Balance

'You want a drink?'
Jon pulled a fifth of Scotch
from the faux marble desk drawer.
We slaved in tan cubicles.
He was real
in a sea of
fake.

Sales Jerks

'Brainwashed?' Bill said
and slipped on his
$300 designer shoes.
'I do what I want,' he sneered.
'Morons are easily influenced,
not me.'

Real College

In college
I was *THE* writer
Students praised
my talent
The cold water came
after submitting
to the City Paper
Rejected
Rewritten
Repeat

Office Speak

'Be proactive,' the CEO said.
'What's proactive mean?'
He frowned.
'In favor of active?' I said.
Want ads had evolved
to online job lists.

Resist the Urge

I won't write haiku
Warm rain against the window
The pen's ink runs dry
(Damn.)

Interview

'What are your goals?'
the boss said
as the blue necktie
contoured his gut.
'Someday I'll die.
Does that count?'
I didn't get
the job.

Indentured

'Get to work.'
'Ok.'
'You're no Steve King, but fine.'
High praise, I supposed.
Gotta buy the boy clothes.
Gotta pay the bills.
Gotta eat.

Workday Evenings

The drinking turned ugly
when the price of Jack
stayed the same
but grew too expensive
Bitter cheap whiskey
is a natural companion
to lunacy

Saturday Morning Thoughts

Family strife
the pursuit of loot
and wild women
social pressures
fitness
and faith
in one true God
Sleep in, baby
You deserve a rest

Awakening

The world has tried
without fail
to whip me like a
corporate bum
It's my turn
now
to wrap leather
around my fist
and rectify
that imbalance

Resist Plutocracy

No one wants to sell
shiny trinkets
but too many people
give greed a higher value
than freedom
Workplaces
incubate
tyranny
We must
FIGHT

Drunken Slumber

'Drink up,' Bukowski said
in a dream.
The whiskey tasted angry.
'Am I writing well?'
'Does it pour out of you?'
'Yeah.'
'Good, baby. Drink.'

Work Night Haiku

I drink whiskey
Whiskey in my big belly
No whiskey for you

Desktop Water

When a bottle of water
tastes like a cube wall
you learn to
never drink
what you find
behind a computer screen
no matter
how thirsty
you get

Hard Sell

I once owned a small newspaper.
Selling pizza ads
sucked.
'I don't want an ad. Please leave.'
'Fucking die.'
I wasn't the best
salesman.

Coffee with Linda

'Why freelance writing?' she said.
'No one gets to own me.'
'What about job security?'
'Are you secure?'
She sipped
her coffee
in silence.

The Best Neighbor

'My freelance gig's over.'
Ana didn't respond.
'Writing's tough,' I said.
'Get a new career.'
'Never!'
'I'll cook dinner.'
'I like meat.'

The Right Choice

I almost murdered
my soul
in corporate sales
Those people piss away
their lives
to pay for old age
I chose words,
so I can live
for today

Creative Coaching

Writer's block isn't real
an imagined stress
Take a drink
Look around the room
Find a strange
object or word
Make it happen
I knew you could

Jealousy

Mocked in bars
for writing
by khaki conformists
cube-dwellers
They despise
my corporate escape
and would murder me
if they found
the courage

Honored Voices

I came up on welfare
so I write for the poor
the drywallers
the retail clerks
the ditch diggers
The voices
no one hears
are heard
through me

No Cash, No Troubles

Sometimes you roll the dice, baby
and you pray
You pray hard
You sweat
for that seven
If you're lucky
you get six
you lose
and go home

Know Thyself

Your life
is a shimmering reflection
in a puddle
Study the image
in rippled motion
Determine an ultimate path
Find joy
Fulfill your
destiny

POLITICAL STRIFE

We embrace the poor
Hatred lures us into greed
Everyone loses

Politics 140

Modern politics
is about distractions
on TV
conservative radio
and liberal blogs
It's our job
to turn down
the rhetoric
and follow
the money

Good Government

Welfare sent me
to tech school
The nation
lifted me
from misery
the trenches of poverty
Now I pay taxes
to help others
fulfill their
dreams

Fringe

Most people strive
to be normal
and adapt
to the expectations
of others
The ones who wear
their imagination
as clothing
change the world

Diminution

The stereotypes
all around us
celebrate ignorance
They're responsible for the
erosion of progress
We lose
as they hand power
to the corrupt

Simple Wisdom

'There are three kinds of people,'
dad said as we drove
to the zoo.
'Union men,
men jealous of unions,
and rich bastards.'
I never
forgot.

Experience

Never doubt
those who live in hardship
know exactly
how the world works
The poor support
their community
The rich hate
their government

Repetition

History is lost
on those who subscribe
to pop values
Suffering of past ages
is ignored
while we forever
repeat the sins
of our ancestors

Foresight

In 10th grade
a boy showed me
a revolver
in his locker.
'The niggers better watch,'
he said.
I knew then,
racism
would define
my generation.

Old Rivals

Pap silently watched
Reagan's funeral
You'd think he mourned
a friend
But pap hated
the union-busting fool
Adversaries
take loss
much harder

Famine

Snack cakes
were once priced
more than beans
Only the rich
can now
eat the earth
The rest of us get fat
on chemicals
while our bodies
starve

Marketing

Republican!
Democrat!
Republican!
Democrat!
Republican!
Democrat!
Slogans remind me of
Tastes great!
Less filling!
Follow money
not madness

Talking Heads

The tea partiers on TV
believe
we are separate
from government
But we are in it together
and must provide
tranquility
to and for
each other

Engagement

The ignorant
who oppose
political discourse
are not enlightened
The American experience
is an ongoing
debate
Freedom is a continual
fight

Young Persuasion

'You're a liberal,'
the gun nut scoffed
and poked me.
'Ok.'
'You should join us.'
I felt like Luke,
facing the dark side
of evil men,
alone.

Pendulum

During dad's time
social justice was
freedom
In the conservative era
business is
freedom
Where the political winds
blow next
is a guess

Propheteering

Political campaigns
are cutthroat
wars of greed
Politicians
use faith
as a sales tool
but truth flourishes
only through defeat
and modesty

Weariness

Be charitable
Criticism of the poor
is easy
evil
The noble resist
temptations of cynicism
even when the greedy
the rich
take and
never share

Delusions

Nuts often scream
the children murdered by guns
never existed
Parents weep as
assault weapons
remain more valuable
than truth
or sanity

Grit

Survival of the fittest
is a lonely road
reserved for honored
champions
The weak and greedy
they choose deception
to overcome
challenges

Furor

In Amsterdam
a moviegoer can order
a glass of beer
and drink it
during a film
We'd smash the mug
in a drunken revolt
and weaponize
a shard

Broken

Four cops
beat a bum
to tears
with night sticks.
A guy at the bar said
'he deserved it.'
The cops were fired.
The bum
became a crippled
bum.

Desolation

The father
who desperately
seeks ways to
feed his family
in poverty
is far more dangerous
and far more honorable
than any CEO
or politician

Searching

Explorers
seek knowledge
and should be heard
The self-righteous
who already know truth
spend their time
convincing others
to shame
explorers

Unbeknownst

Traditionalists grasp
at the last threads of
institutionalized hatred
Their shadow
contrasts the light
to reveal
a narrow path
of progress

Imagine

On Earth
greed throttles
imagination
as Voyager sails
through space
The probe slipped past
the greasy trough
to fulfill
our desire
to learn

Power

As cowards shop
in stores
with assault weapons
on their backs
I remember
what pap used to say:
'The evil man
with the biggest stick
rules.'

Optimism

In the midst of hatred
and despair
angels counteract
the evil
that threatens
to consume us all
We must only
open our minds
to sense them

FRIENDS
AND
ENEMIES

I called in the night
Five conjured ways to say no
You jumped in the car

Camaraderie

Men lose friends
with age
Family becomes the
priority
along with stubborn pride
But friends provide us
release
Friends keep men young

Fishing Boat

Tim would look up at dusk.
'Sam, ever see a sky that orange?'
He'd ask over
and over
until Sam went mad.
'Fuck you!'
We laughed
every time.

Sweet Reward

When the drunk wants a fight
buck up and roll the dice
Win or lose
the best woman in the joint
tastes sweeter
with blood on your lip

In Her Honor

'I busted the bitch in her lip.'
'The bitch is my friend.'
'But she hung on that dude!'
The coward dropped
with the thud of
concrete mix.

Self-Determination

> Joe married Beth,
> despite our warnings
> Cocaine flowed
> and bills went unpaid
> through the divorce
> Sometimes experience
> trumps wise advice

Life Happens

> Our group filled
> summer weekends
> with fishing
> and camping
> Weekends are now
> lonely
> People dissipate as smoke
> All that remains
> are memories

Coffeehouse Bathroom

While writing, a college girl
walked out of a nearby can.
'You were in there a while,' I said.
'You're not funny.'
'Yes, I am.'
'Fuck off.'

Waiting Room

During car repairs
an old man talked to me.
'My wife won't do me,'
he said
'and I'm super nice.'
'Stop being nice,'
I said,
'and fuck her.'

Free Insult

A writer approached me.
'Pittsburgh sucks,' she said.
'Fuck you.'
'Can you help me publish?'
'Nope,' I said,
'I'll get suck all over it.'

Inappropriate

A businessman sat next to me
at the coffeehouse.
'You make money writing?'
'A gazillion dollars.'
'That's sarcasm.'
'Very good!'
He left.

Road Rage

A yuppie blew his BMW horn at me
for driving slow.
'Hair mousse emergency?' I yelled.
'Fuck you, granny!'
'Pull over!'
He sped off.
Coward.

Fill in the Rest

Smoke rose from the gun
on the floor
near the broken lamp
Blood oozed from his forehead
The only present emotion
as breath escaped me
relief

Skillz

You take one on the jaw
give one to the gut
Blood is pure salt
We fight for senseless pride
for honor
but a man
must be good
at something

Outgoing Introvert

I'm a writer
therefore
I find people
partly fascinating
partly disgusting
and partly annoying
Guess which one defines you
Exactly

Friendly Advice

You always sweat it
but it can't be controlled
Suck up those tears and
form a wicked smile
Life's ride will be over
far sooner than
you expect

Cautious Devotion

Unconditional love is not
obligatory
and obligatory love is not
unconditional
Please
baby
don't hurt the ones
you need

Education

'You'll be tough someday,'
the fire chief said.
'How will I know?'
'When you wipe blood from your lip.'
'With a skinned knuckle?'
He smiled.

Haiku Booze Break

The drunken misfit
Disrespected and forgotten
More whiskey for one

Frenemy

'I don't read,' he said.
I asked, 'Why?'
'Makes me tired.'
'The right book
will keep you engaged.'
'Eh, I'll see the movie.'
Bastard.

Night Fishing

'Skunk!' Roy said.
He turned his flashlight
to reveal a picnic table
next to the lake.
We laughed,
but each of us breathed
silent relief.

May Days

Highway driving
Laughter
The sun's warmth
Cool breeze
through open windows
Proof of God's existence
and his absolute
devotion

Poor Choices

I'm your complete stranger
but a better friend
than the guy you've known 20 years
Remember that when choosing
quantity over quality

Lacking Clout

'You shoot pool?'
'No, I don't shoot pool.'
'Then I don't trust you.'
'Why, because I don't shoot pool?'
'Because you don't belong here.'

Disappointment

'The jerk blew me off,' Ana said.
'He's probably a date rapist.'
She glared at me.
'I'm done with men.'
'I still love ya.'
That didn't help.

BLOOD IS THICKER THAN RAGE

'Happy Thanksgiving!'
'You deserve to burn in Hell.'
'You're probably right.'

Blood, Always

Living among family
is a constant barrage
of chaos
love
and guilt
We hope and search
for tranquility
only to discover
it does not
exist

Summer Sundays

Dad's softball games
were fun
until I had to poo.
He pulled down my shorts
and sat me in grass.
'Go.'
'No.'
We left early.
He laughed
later.

Special Treat

Pap sometimes took me to
McDonald's
after Mass.
Gram always shook her head.
'Why do you take him there?'
Pap shrugged.
'He's my grandson.'

Gandy

'I have a surprise,'
mom said.
I parked my bike.
She opened the door
and out ran a puppy.
That Doberman
loved me
through all the
tough times

Real Conversation

'Dad, I hate school.'
'I know.'
'Why should I go?'
'Because I have to work.'
'You get paid.'
'You're right.'
I'd never been right
before.

Just Chit-Chat

'I have emphysema,'
gram said to
waitresses
in diners.
'I'm so sorry,'
they'd reply.
Gram didn't have
emphysema.
She thrived on
sympathy.

Rage

'You gave him cake?'
mom roared at gram
over the phone.
'We're going to fight!'
Her rage
meant the hitting
would soon begin.
I never cried.

Confined Universe

Enduring the love
of a mentally-ill parent
alone
is to live confined
inside tragic
performance art
a theme of
unpredictable rage
and sadness

Distance

'You're wearing a suit,' I said.
Dad stared through the windshield
at nothing.
'I'm getting married.'
'You didn't tell me.'
'I know. Sorry.'

Learning Curve

I never knew how to be a
big brother
I showed him
violent movies
and taught him about
women
The toddler who laughed
at me
grew up
just fine

Stepmothers

'What happened to my room?' I said.
'It's a guest room.'
'My toys?'
'Put away.'
'Can I have them?'
'No.'
Dad visited with me
less often.

9 Weeks In Prison

Report card days
were trials.
'This isn't honor roll.'
'Sorry, mom.'
'No TV and no outside.'
I always counted
the years until
I turned 18.

Depression

Mom gave me Gandy
as insulation
from her madness
I needed a best friend
a distraction
from her quiet
sobs
obnoxious rage
and streaming
tears

Badass

Dogs shit behind the shed
until Gram stepped
in a pile
She shoveled their turds
and dumped them
in the dog owner's yard
Shit never
returned

Lifecycle

As a kid
I couldn't wait to
grow up
When the work alarm
jolted me awake at 6am
I wished back
to pap's coos
for breakfast
and cartoons

Forgotten

Family life
is a stank prison
to the young
Pushing family aside
for selfish desires
is a freeing sensation
before loneliness
drives madness

Disclosure

Gram lay in the hospice,
her soul tortured,
days numbered.
'I had a daughter,'
she revealed,
'before your mom.'
It hurt her
to admit
truth

Malevolence

When a parent
condemns you to Hell
for their unfulfilled wishes
they suffer torment
Their misery desires
companionship
your company

Imitation

I snort
when I laugh
Friends tease me
Pap snorted
at comedians on TV
What worked for the man
who gave me sanity
faith
guidance
works for me

Fatherly Advice

"When you get paid,"
one uncle told me,
"pay yourself first."
I stood quiet,
absorbing his wisdom.
"No one ever taught you that?"
"Nope."

The Routine

Pap went to Mass
every
single
day.
I went Sundays
We never dressed up
Sometimes we'd snicker
at people in suits
We called them
tourists

Property Rights

'I'll give you my old computer,'
I told a cousin,
'for your kids.'
Mom's demons overheard.
Her swift kicks
to the balls
changed my mind.

My Firefighter

You've got guts
The charred house smokes
Another life saved
The boy I made
is grown
As you remove your helmet
please know
I watched
in pride

LIFE OR DEATH
EVERLASTING

The righteous man kneels
and humbly requests the strength
to fight for what's right

Self-Inflicted

Sometimes before bed
I pray in a rush
as a chore
On those nights
I sleep in torture
and awake groggy
wondering why
I didn't seek
true peace

Silent Miracle

Our 5th grade choir
sung a song
for the mother of God
The teacher promised
Mary would remember us
for paying such tribute
She always has

Divorce

'Dad, will you go to Heaven?'
'Yeah, why do you ask?'
'You and mom are divorced.'
He shot me
a crooked smile
of concern
'God loves us all.'

In Service

'Why do you want to be an altar boy?'
my priest said.
'It'd be fun.'
'Better than sitting still?'
'Yes.'
He laughed
in delight
at my
honesty

Heavenly Ruse

People ask if I'm destined
for Heaven or Hell
I'll trick the devil
into believing
my ass is on fire
while begging
angels to open
the gates

Validation

Parents hug for love
Lovers hug for intimacy
But after a long struggle
a role model's embrace
is the embodiment
of God's honor
given to you

Observation

Witnessing others suffer
personal hells
of sick minds
delivers to us
a distinct understanding
of madness
of evil
and the narrow path
to God

Exploration

Some people say
the universe will
soon end
No father
would give his children
a book
and take it away
before they've read
the last page

Goodbye

I read to pap
as tubes ran from his mouth.
He looked at me.
I closed the book.
'You were the best pap.'
He nodded.
His eyes said
I love you.

True Peace

When I consider the souls
of loved ones
in Heaven
chaos and rage
around me
vanishes
Air is cleaner
and sounds are joyful
in those moments

Precariousness

'I gave up faith,'
Ana said,
'after dad died.
Death is so senseless.'
I sat there
silent
I should've told her
it's us who give life
meaning.

Temptation

One night
in a moment of despair
I asked angels
to rescue me
Sinister intents
took control
Regret of human
failure
has haunted me
ever after

Spiral

Terror strikes at the heart
when creeping darkness
chokes out raging thoughts
Madness then comes to the surface
making escape impossible

Spiritual Incursion

On a moonless night
evil attacked me
behind the tavern
It wormed through flesh
and invaded my soul
until I embodied
its darkness
its hatred

Premeditation

I lunge the blade
deep into your gut
Warmth fills each crevice
of my hand
Satisfaction is relief
as your residue
your evil
washes away
gone

Gram's Funeral Stress

'Is the wake ready?'
mom said from her car.
'Yeah.'
'That woman tortured me.'
'I know.'
She then started
the engine
and shot me
the finger.

Autumn

No one can deny the beauty
of colorful leaves
But days grow short and
chilled air carries the
scent of decay
It seems odd
that we
rejoice

Last Words

'That girl I dated,'
I said,
'is pregnant.'
Dad worked on the mower
in silence.
'It's not yours,'
he finally said.
Six weeks later,
he died.

Haiku of Loss

Memories in a picture
Our best conversations lost
The box smells of you

Pap's Wish

'When I die,'
pap said over Sunday coffee,
'tell them I loved
Christ and the Virgin Mother.'
'I wanted to give a eulogy.'
'No.'
We both won.

Suicide by Procreation

Overtime at the job
you hate
Homework and heart stress
Worry drives madness
Drugs and resentment
These are the tools
for an early
demise

Sorrowful

When death comes
I'll be comforted to know
my passing carried no great shock
and little consequence
to those who claimed
affection for me

Viral Perspective

Incurable illness
is a community's
best friend
when it takes hold
in an otherwise healthy
psychopath
Some diseases
deserve our
respect

Dream Vanquish

A gangster
reached over the driver's seat
and dragged a blade
across my throat
I fought back until
he fled
Bad asses don't die
in nightmares

Struggle

Forever madness
Gunpowder smells of surrender
Rain on the window
Chaos will soon be gone
Blood oozes
tickles my cheek
Torment fades
to black

No Exit

'You're going to Hell!'
A mother's screams
for your eternal
damnation
hurt worse
than her nails
dug into your face.
Escape is
impossible.

Perdition

What do you see
when you close your eyes
and creeping madness approaches?
I hear the screams of
lost souls,
but can't see
a damn thing

Superbia

Wars are only waged
by the corrupt
When a man kneels
with a true spirit
his pride
his egotism
evaporates
as morning dew
under God's sun

I Confess to You 140

I confess to God
I have sinned
in thoughts and words
in actions and apathy
I ask blessed Mary
all the angels and saints
and you
Pray for me

The Final MicroPoem

'Why all the tweets?' Ana said.
'They're MicroPoems.'
'Are you writing this conversation?'
'No.'
'Yes, you are.'
'Can I have food?'
'Fine.'

That's the end, my friend
You don't have to go home
but you can't stay here

About the Author

Ron Gavalik is a writer
in Pittsburgh, Pennsylvania.
You can stalk him online.
He likes whiskey.

Made in the USA
Middletown, DE
07 March 2022

62228088R00066